GROWING UP
ALONE

Front cover: *A baby scarlet king snake breaks out from its egg ready to face the world. Its mother laid her eggs in a sheltered place, perhaps under some rocks, and went off, never to see her babies hatch and grow up.*

Created and Produced by Firecrest Books Ltd
in association with John Francis/Bernard Thornton Artists

Copyright © 2001 Firecrest Books Ltd
and Copyright © 2001 John Francis/Bernard Thornton Artists

Published by Tangerine Press™, an imprint of Scholastic Inc.
555 Broadway, New York, NY 10012

Tangerine Press™ and associated logo and design are trademarks of Scholastic Inc.

ISBN 0-439-30532-2

Printed and bound in Belgium
First printing, September 2001

GROWING UP
ALONE

Bernard Stonehouse

Illustrated by
John Francis

TANGERINE PRESS™ and associated logo
and design are trademarks of Scholastic Inc.

FOR VELLANGANI AND
ALL THE OTHER ORPHANS
OF THE WORLD

Art and Editorial Direction by
Peter Sackett

Designed by
Paul Richards, Designers & Partners

Edited by
Norman Barrett

Color separation by
Sang Choy International Pte. Ltd.
Singapore

Printed and bound by
Casterman, Belgium

CONTENTS

Introduction

As humans, we are used to the idea that parents look after their children – in our case for many years – before the children are grown up enough to look after themselves. In the animal world, caring parents usually tend and defend eggs and young against attacks by predators, and lead their chicks, cubs, calves, or pups away from all kinds of dangers. Just by going about their daily business, they act as examples or role models from which their young can learn.

Not all animals arrange their lives this way. This newly hatched tortoise, for example, will never see its parents. It will grow up alone, and probably be none the worse for it. As a reptile, its brain is strong on instincts, or built-in behavior, but weak on learning. A baby turtle would not learn much from parental examples. Many, indeed most, invertebrate animals, from starfish to spiders, produce offspring that grow up far from their parents, in completely different environments. Chances of survival, at least for a few of these young, are better without their parents than with them. This book tells of 20 assorted animals that, for one reason or another, leave their offspring to grow up alone.

Common dogfish

Walk along an ocean beach after a storm, and you may find what are known as mermaid's purses. They are usually empty, but just occasionally you'll see one filled with an oily yolk and a tiny, half-formed fish. These are the eggs of a particular kind of dogfish.

Dogfish are small, spotted sharks, which grow up to about 4 feet (1.2 m) long, that live in shallow, northern coastal seas of both Europe and the Americas. There are several different kinds. Sailors called them dogfish because they seem to hunt in packs like wild dogs. Where there is one, there are usually hundreds, and tens of thousands are caught by fishermen every year.

Some kinds of fish produce hundreds of tiny eggs at a time, in masses that look like spotted jelly. Others produce just a few large eggs, each packaged in a shell with a yolk for the growing embryo to feed on. Spotted dogfish lay eggs of this kind. The shell is horny, with a tendril at each corner that tangles with seaweed and holds the egg down. That way it is less likely to be seen and eaten by other fish. The little dogfish that breaks out of the egg is all ready to look after itself right from the start.

Just out of the egg, the tiny dogfish carries a yolk sac that provides it with a few days' food.

Dogfish lay their eggs among seaweed, which hides them from predators. When washed up on the beach, the eggs are called mermaid's purses.

Mason wasp

On a warm, sandy cliff face you will sometimes see hundreds of little tubes, half an inch (1 cm) or so long, with tiny wasplike insects buzzing in and out of them. The insects are mason wasps, and the tubes form the entrances to their nests.

A mason is a person who carves stone for buildings or statues. Mason wasps carve and mold sand to make holes for their nests. It has to be sand of a particular texture, neither so hard that the wasps cannot carve it, nor so soft that it caves in. Using their strong jaws and front legs, the wasps carve out tunnels in the cliff face, and mold some of the sand with sticky saliva to make the tubes. Then they go hunting. Each female mason wasp hunts for tiny caterpillars. When she finds one of the right size and shape, she injects it with a drop of liquid that paralyzes it and puts it to sleep. Then she picks it up in her jaws, flies with it back to the nest, and places it carefully in the tunnel, pushing it back to the end. Then she flies off to find another one. When she has gathered three or four caterpillars, she lays an egg among them and leaves the nest altogether, sealing the entrance with sand. She makes several such nests in a single summer before she dies.

After a few days, the egg hatches, and the wasp larva starts to feed on the caterpillars. The larva never sees either of its parents. It grows quickly, and the three or four caterpillars provide just enough food for it to mature and change into an adult wasp.

The adult wasp catches caterpillars, carries them to her nest, and lays an egg among them.

The wasp larva hatches and eats its way through the caterpillar food store.

There is just enough food for the larva to turn into an adult wasp.

Caddis fly

Under stones in a clear freshwater stream in summer, you may find caddis fly larvae. They are usually small, up to half an inch (1 cm) long. Use a magnifying glass to see them properly. Each larva lives in a case made of sand grains, slivers of wood, or vegetation, sticking firmly to the underside of the stone. If you lift a stone out to examine the larvae, try to put it back just exactly where you found it, or the larvae may die.

Adult caddis flies are flying insects with furry wings and bodies. They flutter over the water like moths on warm, sunny evenings. There are hundreds of different kinds. They lay strands of eggs on the surface of the water or attached to plant stems. The eggs hatch into tiny larvae that sink to the bottom and attach themselves to stones. As soon as they have settled, the larvae start to feed by filtering algae and other living fragments from the water. They also collect material for their protective cases, adding more as they grow. This helps to hide them and protect them from predators. After one or two summers, the larvae turn into pupae, then into adult caddis flies.

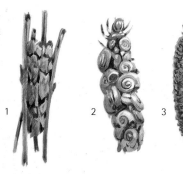

Different species of larvae make their cases from different materials – (1) grains of sand, twigs, and other debris, (2) snail shells, and (3) sand and grit.

1   2   3

The eggs hatch into larvae, which grow for a year or more, pupate, and turn into adult flies.

Dor beetle

When a horse, cow, sheep, or antelope has eaten and digested grass, there is often a lot of nourishment left in the dung that they release. Several different kinds of beetles live almost entirely on dung of this kind. They not only feed on it themselves, but lay their eggs in it to make sure that their young get a good head start.

These particular dung beetles, called dor beetles, fly into a new patch of droppings. Using their front feet, they mold it into balls like cooks making meatballs. Then they roll the balls, pushing with their strong hind legs (main picture), to places where the ground is soft enough for them to dig holes. Each beetle scoops out a system of tunnels, pushes two or three of the balls into the tunnels, and then backfills with soil. Each of the balls will contain one of its own eggs.

When the egg hatches, the new larva finds itself with a good food supply of dung – that is, partly digested and decaying vegetation just right for it to feed on. It never knows its parents. By the time it has eaten its way through the dung, it is ready to pupate, transform into a beetle, and later become a parent itself.

Dor beetles roll their balls of dung into holes in the ground and lay an egg in each.

This cross section shows the balls of dung, each with an egg, safely stored at the ends of passages in the tunnel.

The larva, like a hairy caterpillar, eats steadily through the dung balls, growing and eventually changing into an adult flying beetle.

Eastern box turtle

Turtles are tortoises that live in or very near to water. Nearly all tortoises and turtles, when they are attacked or threatened, pull their head and legs into their shell for safety. Box turtles have hinges on the underside that allow them to close the shell almost completely, like a box. This makes them even safer from predators.

Eastern box turtles live in the southeastern corner of the United States, usually in damp, marshy ground. They grow to about 6 inches (15 cm) long. In warm weather they are lively little animals, scuffling through the leaves and undergrowth, seeking out the insects, worms, and berries that are their main food. When danger threatens, they pull in their head and limbs and close the box. It is a simple life.

At breeding time in early spring, males and females come together and mate. The females scrape deep holes in the sand and lay 20 or more white eggs, which they cover and leave. A few weeks later the little turtles break their way out of the eggs, using a special egg tooth on their nose, and come up to the surface. There is enough yolk left over to feed them for a few days. But usually they are feeding and fending for themselves within hours of hatching.

Eggs laid in damp sand hatch without help or attention from the parents. The little turtles emerge and set off alone.

A hinged undershell allows the box turtle to close itself up completely.

Diamondback rattlesnake

Here a young rattlesnake, about 12 inches (30 cm) long, that was born just over an hour ago. Its mother slid off as soon as it was born. It won't see her again. Equipped with poison fangs, it has already started catching lizards, mice, and other small prey, though it is still too young to have a rattle of its own.

There are a dozen different kinds of rattlesnakes in North America, living mostly on the drier plains where cattle and horses graze. Snakes in general make almost no sounds –

just a quiet *hiss-ss-ss* when they are disturbed. But adult rattlesnakes carry rattles in their tails that you can hear 6 to 10 feet (2 to 3 m) away. Biologists think that the rattle is a warning, useful in reminding the big mammals not to tread accidentally on the snakes.

Rattlesnakes produce eggs, but keep them inside their bodies until they hatch, so their young are born alive. A female rattlesnake 5 feet (1.5 m) long may give birth to between 10 and 20 tiny offspring. Once they emerge, neither the mother nor her mate have anything to do with their babies. At first, the young snakes have no rattle. As they grow, they shed their skin two or three times a year, and the rattle builds up from segments of dried tail skin.

The rattle is formed from segments of dry tail skin. Young rattlesnakes have small rattles . . .

. . . that grow larger every time they shed their skin.

Black-headed duck

Most ducks incubate clutches of eight to 12 eggs in warm, well-lined nests. Both parents tend their young carefully, giving the ducklings a good start in their first weeks of life. The ducklings learn a lot from their parents about feeding and staying safe.

The black-headed diving duck, which lives in the rain forests of South America, manages her young quite differently. She lays her eggs one at a time in other ducks' nests, leaving them to be raised by foster parents. The ducklings hatch and are cared for by their foster families, but never know their own parents.

Why should this be? We don't know enough about them to be sure. Several other kinds of birds – for example, common cuckoos – lay their eggs in other birds' nests. It saves the mothers all the energy of nest-building and chick-rearing, and those that do so have time and energy to lay more eggs than they otherwise would. Cuckoo chicks grow faster than those of their hosts, and win out in feeding.

Black-headed ducks may succeed in a similar way. They lay big eggs, resulting in big, strong chicks. When food is scarce, the big black-headed ducklings will perhaps be able to compete successfully with their smaller foster brothers and sisters, so more will survive.

Black-headed ducks swim at the surface, but dive and catch their food underwater.

The black-headed duck lays a big egg, producing a big chick (below right), which outgrows other chicks in the nest.

Mallee fowl

Mallee fowls are big birds, about the size of domestic hens. They live in Australia, in areas of dry shrubs and desert. They feed mainly on insects. Males build huge nests (see upper picture, below left), 12 feet (3.7 m) across and more than 8 feet (2.4 m) deep – bigger nests than any other bird builds. Starting more than a year ago, it took the male two months to dig a pit in the sandy soil, and another eight months to fill it with leaves, which the spring rains helped to rot. The nest has turned into a compost heap, generating its own heat. The mallee fowl from time to time tested the temperature with his bill. When the heap was warm enough, he courted a mallee fowl hen, who came and laid about six white eggs in it. They covered the eggs with leaves and sand, and left them to incubate (see picture below left).

The male has been back every day, testing the temperature to keep it level at about 91°F (33°C), so that the eggs neither chill nor cook. Now one of the chicks (main picture) has hatched and popped out of the heap. In a moment it will race off into the bushes for safety. It is completely independent, and will never see or know its parents or learn anything from them.

If the heap warms, the male mallee opens it to let the heat out. If it cools, he scratches more soil over it.

This cross section shows the nest with the eggs resting on a warm layer of rotting leaves, which is covered with sand.

Common kiwi

Despite their name, common kiwis are not particularly common in the wild. To see one, you need to be in just the right place at the right time. The right place is New Zealand's rain forest. The right time is late evening or night, because that is when they are most active. Even on their home grounds there are not many of them. You are more likely to hear them than to see them, snuffling and scratching on the forest floor. Related to ostriches, though very much smaller, they stand about 16 inches (41 cm) tall and weigh up to 7 pounds (3.2 kg). They cannot fly – their wings are tiny stubs, tucked away under those long body feathers. The long, tubular bill is a sensitive feeler and probe for finding the earthworms and insect larvae that are their main food.

Even harder to find are their nests. Hens lay one big egg, sometimes two, in a cave or hollow. Only the cocks (which are smaller than the hens) incubate the eggs, for about 10 weeks. When the chick hatches, it stays in the nest for four or five days without feeding, then walks away and starts to probe for worms. Father may follow, but he doesn't seem to feed the chick or show it any tricks for living.

Kiwis lay one or two very large eggs (one shown here for size), which the males alone incubate.

Downy chicks look after themselves as soon as they leave the nest, hiding in corners to keep out of danger.

Common lobster

This young lobster with huge eyes is sinking down to the bottom of the sea, not far from the shore. In the dim light among the seaweed 100 feet (30 m) down, hungry fish and other enemies will find it hard to see the greenish-gray shell, and those legs and antennae

The eggs float to the surface (1) and hatch into tiny, glassy larvae (2).

1

2

will look like strands of weed. It will find a small hollow or cave, where it can sit facing outward, watching and feeling with its antennae for food drifting past. If it sees or feels something moving, it will jump out and pounce, grabbing with those pincers and crunching with small but strong jaws.

Only a few weeks old, it has already traveled many miles from where it began as an egg. Its mother, a mature female lobster, produced several dozen small, translucent eggs, carrying them for a few days on her body. The eggs ripened, detached, and floated off, rising to the sea surface. There they hatched into tiny, transparent larvae, which drifted with the currents and tides. They fed on even tinier animals and plant cells that drifted with them. Gradually they grew and changed, passing through crablike stages before turning into this large-eyed stage – something that looks much more like a lobster. Now it is time to return to the seabed. Many miles from where it began, this youngster knows nothing of its mother, who has no idea of what has happened to this or any other of her young.

The fully grown lobster develops much bigger claws and a stronger body.

Garden tiger moth

Hungry birds like to hunt among the leaves for caterpillars. This particular kind of caterpillar, called a woolly bear, would be bad news for any bird that tried to eat it. It is covered in prickly fur, and it may contain poisons that would give the bird indigestion or worse – perhaps even kill it. Birds that peck at woolly bears quickly learn not to bother them, but to keep hunting and find something else more palatable instead.

Woolly bears are the caterpillars of a particular kind of moth called garden tiger moths. These are quite common in both Europe and the United States. Brightly colored, with brilliant tiger-striped wings, the moths fly during the long summer evenings. Males and females find each other by scent, and the females lay tiny eggs on the leaves of a wide range of shrubs. The caterpillars hatch a few days later, never seeing or knowing their parents.

Tiny at first, they grow quickly, munching the leaves on which they hatch, then moving on to find others. Sometimes thousands of them hatch and grow together, eating all the leaves off hundreds of shrubs, and crossing roads and railway lines in search of more food. Then each caterpillar turns into a pupa, or chrysalis, emerging as a moth in the following spring.

You sometimes see thousands of woolly bear caterpillars together, growing bigger (1) and bigger (2) as they eat the leaves from bushes and other plants.

1

2

Adult tiger moths have vivid patches on their forewings and brightly colored hind wings, warning birds that, like their caterpillars, they are not good to eat.

Ant lion (doodlebug)

An ant lion is not an ant, and nothing like a lion. It is a strange little buglike larva – that is, a young form that grows into a different-looking adult. It lives in sandy soil. Just looking at it, you might never guess what kind of adult it turns into. Its parents were delicate flies, something like small dragonflies, with two lacy wings on either side of a long, slender body. That is what this squat, hairy little doodlebug will become in another year or so.

Meanwhile, it is an ant lion, with a life of its own to live. It started as an egg, which hatched into a small larva, which has grown in stages to this larger one, less than half an inch (1 cm) long. It has dug itself a pit in firm sand, and is sitting at the bottom, waiting for prey to fall in. The prey may be an ant or a small fly. Whatever it is, the ant lion will reach forward and grab it with those scissorlike mandibles, injecting poison that will paralyze and kill the prey. Then the ant lion will suck out its juices, throw the body out of the pit with a toss of its head, and wait for its next victim to fall in.

Too fat to walk far, the ant lion larva has thin, spindly legs that help to anchor it in the pit.

The larva turns into a pupa (resting stage), then into a delicate, lacy-winged fly (left).

Goose barnacle

A baby goose barnacle (bottom picture) is a tiny animal less than 0.1 inch (0.25 cm) long, with a spiny transparent shell, beady eyes, and lots of legs. It lives at the sea surface along with thousands of other small animals, looking like the larva, or young form, of a lobster (see page 26). After several changes it turns not into a lobster, but into a goose barnacle, as shown in the main picture, on the right.

Goose barnacles, 2 to 3 inches (5 to 7.5 cm) long, live in clusters on logs and seaweed floating on the sea surface, or even on whales. The hard outer shell, with a hinged opening, makes them look like some kind of stalked mussel or oyster. In fact, they are crustaceans, more closely related to lobsters and shrimp than to geese or mussels.

Inside that hard outer case is a little animal that looks like the front half of a shrimp. It seems to be standing on its head and waving its legs, but the legs set up a current that draws water and food into the shell so that the shrimplike barnacle can feed. When the time comes, the barnacle can release eggs from its shell into the water. The eggs drift away far from the parent and hatch into larval forms that allow them to feed at the water's surface.

Inside the goose barnacle shell is a little animal that looks like part of a tiny shrimp.

Each egg turns into a larva that eventually settles and turns into a barnacle.

Gila monster

This is a fully grown female gila (say "hee-lah") monster, about 2 feet (60 cm) long, warming herself in a patch of sunshine in a desert of the southwestern United States. She is not really a monster – just a reptile with a bad reputation for giving poisonous bites. A more polite name is beaded lizard, because the skin is covered with scales like tiny glass beads.

Last week she scraped a nest bowl in a nearby sand patch, laid a clutch of two dozen white eggs in it, and covered them over with sand. Just a few inches below the surface, the eggs are kept at a warm, steady temperature by the sand. Soon they will hatch – two dozen tiny gila monsters. Each about 8 inches (20 cm) long, they will break from their shells, push their way through the sand, and emerge into the world. Each hatchling has the last remnants of an egg yolk, which will feed it for a few days. Very soon it will have to start hunting on its own, looking particularly for small birds, mice, or other reptiles, which it will kill it with an injection of poison from its lower jaw. As it grows, it will kill bigger prey.

Even a half-grown gila monster carries enough poison to give a nasty and painful bite. Never mess with one of any size.

Gila monsters lay their eggs in sand, covering and leaving them as soon as they are laid.

The bright colors of both babies (left) and adults (below) are a do-not-touch warning to other animals.

Atlantic horseshoe crab

They are called crabs, and like true crabs they have hard shells and live in the sea. But these horseshoe crabs, up to 2 feet (0.6 m) long, are more closely related to spiders and scorpions than to crabs or lobsters. Many more species lived in the past than are alive today, some much bigger and others smaller than the ones shown here.

As adults, Atlantic horseshoe crabs live in deep water along the coast of North America. In the breeding season they come in the thousands into shallow waters just offshore. Males and females pair, and at high tide the females dig pits in the sand with their shovellike shells. They lay up to 1,000 eggs, which the males fertilize with sperm before covering them over with sand. Then the adults return to deep water. The eggs take several weeks to hatch, and the tiny larvae escape from their pits to go their own way. They feed on tiny algae and other small particles of living or recently dead material, growing slowly. As they grow bigger, two or three times yearly they burst from their old shell and grow a new one. It takes them at least nine years to reach adult size and shape, and become parents themselves.

Independent from first hatching (above), the young horseshoe crabs quickly come to look like adults (below), but take nine or 10 years to reach full adult size (main picture).

Red salamander

Long, narrow bodies and short legs make these salamanders look like lizards. However, there are important differences. Salamanders are amphibians, related to frogs, toads, and newts, with moist smooth skins. Lizards are reptiles, with dry, scaly skin. Reptiles can live in very dry places, even in deserts. Amphibians have to live in water, or in very damp places close to water. Why? Because they breathe partly or mainly through their skin, and must stay damp to keep up their supply of oxygen.

This red salamander is one of many dozens of species that live in the United States. If they came out by day, salamanders as bright as this would almost certainly be snapped up by predatory birds or snakes. So they emerge mainly at night, into a cool, watery world where they hunt for tiny insects and slugs, usually finding them by scent. They hatched from eggs that were laid in damp, mossy ground at the edges of ponds and streams. The eggs turned into larvae with feathery gills, which feed and grow without further help from their parents. The gills disappear after a few weeks, leaving bright red young salamanders that darken as they grow older.

Red salamanders lay their eggs on damp ground close to water.

The young larval salamanders hatch with a supply of food in a yolk sac . . .

. . . older larvae have feathery gills that help them to breathe.

Atlantic salmon

Salmon eggs are laid in pink, jellylike masses on the streambed and fertilized by the males. The eggs hatch into tiny salmon that make their way back to the sea, growing all the time.

Here is a big male salmon, fighting his way upriver against a strong current. He is nearly there – only a few more miles to go, and he'll be in a much quieter stretch of water. There will be dozens of other big salmon, male and female, all ready to breed. The females will lay masses of pink, jelly-covered eggs among the gravel (see picture on the left), and the males will fertilize them with sperm. Then both parents will drift downstream, back to the sea.

The eggs will hatch, and the young larvae will float away, feeding first on yolk from the sac attached to their body, then on tiny insect larvae from the streambed. Gradually, they will find their way down the river to the ocean, feeding and fattening as they go. In the ocean they will spend three or four years. After one year they will be 2 feet (0.6 m) long, after three years about 3 feet (0.9 m) long and weighing 17 pounds (8 kg), possibly more. In their third, fourth, or fifth year they will return to the river where they were hatched, and fight their way upstream against the current – just like the big male on the right. If possible they will find the very stream and gravel bed where they began.

Three stages in the life of young salmon: They are known as fry (1) in their first year, parr (2) in their second, and then as smolt (3).

American bullfrog

The little animals pictured below with long tails are different stages of tadpoles – the young or larval forms of a frog. They live in streams in the southeastern United States. In a couple of weeks time they will turn into small American bullfrogs, in smart green-and-yellow coats. In three or four years, they will come to look like the adult bullfrog, up to 6 inches (15 cm) long, as shown in the main picture. Frogs of similar kinds are common in ponds and streams all over the world. Many of them grow from tadpoles that look much like these.

The picture on the left is of a very mature tadpole at a stage just before it turns into a frog. A few weeks ago this tadpole was a tiny black egg, one of hundreds of jelly-covered eggs floating in strings and masses in a backwater of the stream. The eggs developed without any further help or attention from their parents. First, they elongated into small larvae, which broke out of their jelly casing and floated to the surface. Then they developed a large, round head and body and a long flat tail, and began swimming, feeding on tiny green plants in the water. Then they began to grow legs. Soon the tail will disappear, the legs strengthen, and the body take on the shape of the adult frog, ready to leave the water and hop on its new hind legs.

A mature American bullfrog tadpole, with two pairs of legs and a frog-shaped body.

Eggs of an American bullfrog.

Early larval stage with feathers and gills . . .

. . . and the later larval stage with hind legs.

Common snail

Common snails live in warm, damp woodlands and gardens. In wet weather they come out of their shells during the day to browse on the leaves and shoots of green plants. In dry weather they prefer to roam at night, when the air is damper. If the weather turns very dry, they bury themselves under leaves or in the soil, sealing the shell opening and waiting for damp conditions to return.

They breed by laying packages of 40 to 50 fertile eggs a few inches down in the soil. After about seven weeks, the eggs hatch into tiny snails with soft, transparent shells. They feed by grazing on algae and other living organisms from the soil. The shells quickly become chalky and harden. As the soft-bodied snails grow, they add rings to the lip of the shell, so they can always retreat into it.

This kind of snail was once found only in temperate woodlands and gardens of Europe. Now you are just as likely to find them in North America and other parts of the world where there are similar living conditions. Gardeners and farmers sending live plants from Europe to other parts of the world unknowingly sent snail eggs in soil packed around the roots. The eggs survived, and the snails emerged to colonize new continents.

Snails lay eggs in clusters hidden in damp soil.

The newly hatched snail (above) has a thin, transparent shell that quickly hardens as it grows (below).

Crane fly

Here is a crane fly, an insect about 1 inch (2.5 cm) long. It has a single pair of long, thin wings, and six very long, spindly legs. So called because they remind us of long-legged, long-necked birds called cranes, they also have the more popular name "daddy longlegs." There are dozens of species, all closely related, with similar ways of life.

Pictured on the left, also about an inch long, is a leather-jacket. It began as an egg, almost too small to see, laid in the hard, compact soil of a football field. It has strong jaws, and spends its day burrowing through the soil, munching the roots of grasses and other plants. Already a year old, it is fully grown, and will soon become inactive, growing a hard case around itself, and turning into a pupa. After a few weeks the pupa will split, and from it will emerge something quite different – a crane fly.

Crane flies emerge in swarms around late spring and summer, often flying into houses and dancing on the windows. They do not sting or bite. If you find one in a room, it is probably trying to fly out toward the light, and will not hurt you. Catch it in a glass or soft cloth and release it outside.

The leather-jackets (above) that emerge from crane fly eggs feed on the roots of grasses and other plants. They turn into pupae that eventually . . .

. . . change into adult crane flies.

Index

* Caption for front cover